Immigration Reform: Stories, Struggles, and Solutions

Table of Contents

Introduction: Our Broken Immigration System

Immigration has always been a part of human history. People have crossed borders in search of better lives, new opportunities, and safety. Yet, here in the United States, our immigration system is a complex web that often feels more like a tangled mess than a clear pathway. From the moment someone decides to seek a new life in America, they embark on a challenging journey marked by hope, hardship, and often, heartbreak. "Immigration Reform: Stories, Struggles, and Solutions" aims to shed light on this often misunderstood and controversial topic, blending personal stories of real individuals with an analysis of the challenges they face.

Every year, millions of people attempt to navigate a system that's difficult to understand. Many are fleeing violence and persecution, while others are chasing the American Dream—a chance to provide for their families, gain access to education, or simply live in peace. However, the existing policies often seem outdated and counterproductive, leaving many in limbo for years or forcing them into difficult decisions about their futures. This book is an invitation to see beyond the headlines and statistics to grasp the human experiences behind the headlines.

We will explore the historical context of immigration in the U.S., starting from the foundation of the nation up to the present day. You'll meet the faces of the millions affected—children, parents, and the elderly —all navigating the complexities of immigration. Each chapter will unravel a different aspect of our broken system, offering insight into how it affects not only immigrants but also the communities they join.

In the second chapter, we will dive into personal stories of immigrants, showcasing their trials and tribulations and, most importantly, their resilience. These narratives are central to understanding the emotional and psychological weight of the immigration process. Next, we will break down the immigration process itself. What does it really look like to apply for a visa or seek asylum? What hurdles must one overcome, and what kind of support exists? We'll explore these questions in a straightforward manner, making the legal jargon more digestible for everyone.

Furthermore, we cannot ignore the profound impact of our immigration policies on families. In Chapter Four, we will discuss the heartbreaking reality many face, where family members are often separated by borders, bureaucracy, or deportation. This reality invigorates every discussion about immigration and showcases why reforms are so desperately needed.

In Chapters Five and Six, we'll shift focus to refugees and asylum seekers—groups often marginalized in the immigration debate. Many of these individuals come from war-torn countries, fleeing violence and persecution. Their stories remind us that immigration is not only about economics; it's also about humanity. We'll highlight the economic contributions immigrants make to the workforce, dispelling myths and showing the critical roles they play in our society.

As we move toward solutions, Chapters Seven and Eight will focus on advocacy and the paths toward reform. We'll highlight organizations working tirelessly to bridge the gap between immigrants and the resources they need. We will also investigate what a more just and inclusive immigration system might look like and how we can all contribute to making it a reality.

Join me on this journey as we explore our broken immigration system through a lens of empathy and understanding. Together, we can gather insights that not only illuminate the issues at hand but also inspire actions and solutions for a brighter and more inclusive future. Our broken system may seem insurmountable, but through awareness, advocacy, and compassion, we can start to pave the way toward meaningful change.

Chapter 1: The Landscape of Immigration: A Historical Overview

When we think about immigration in the United States, it's easy to get lost in the numbers, statistics, and, at times, heated debates. However, to truly understand where we are today, we need to take a step back and look at our country's history. Immigration has played a crucial role in shaping who we are as a nation. From the very beginning, the United States has been a land of opportunity, drawing people from all corners of the globe. But what does that history tell us? How did we evolve into the system we have now, with its complexities and contradictions?

The Early Years: A Nation of Immigrants

The story of immigration in the U.S. dates back to the arrival of the first settlers in the early 1600s. The Pilgrims and Puritans sought religious freedom, while European countries sent their people to explore and settle new lands. In those early years, the idea of America as a "melting pot" began to emerge. Over the next few centuries, waves of immigrants came from various countries.

Each group brought unique cultures, languages, and traditions, contributing to the rich tapestry of American society.

The 19th century was a particularly transformative time for immigration. The Industrial Revolution created a booming economy, and America needed workers to fill labor shortages. Millions of Europeans, particularly from Ireland and Germany, flocked to the country during this period. They were drawn by the promise of jobs and better living conditions, often risking everything to build new lives. This influx further solidified the U.S. identity as a refuge for those seeking better opportunities.

The Challenges and Changes

However, this rich history wasn't without challenges. As immigration increased, so did the fear and resentment among some existing Americans. Waves of Chinese immigrants arriving in the late 1800s faced severe discrimination and hostility. In response to rising anti-immigrant sentiment, the government enacted laws like the Chinese Exclusion Act of 1882, which effectively barred Chinese laborers from entering the country. This marked the beginning of a trend where political and economic anxieties led to restrictive immigration policies.

Throughout the 20th century, immigration laws continued to evolve. The quota system introduced in the 1920s was a significant turning point. Developed to limit immigrants based on their country of origin, it favored Northern and Western Europeans while virtually excluding those from Asia, Africa, and Southern and Eastern Europe. This system reflected a growing nativism and racism that permeated American society. It wasn't until the 1965 Immigration and

Nationality Act that significant changes occurred, abolishing the quota system and focusing on family reunification and skilled workers.

The Modern Era: Waves of Change

Fast forward to the late 20th and early 21st centuries, and we see new patterns of immigration taking shape. Politically unstable regions, economic crises, and humanitarian issues have caused many to seek refuge in the U.S. Communities from Latin America, the Middle East, and Africa have grown, often bringing vibrant cultures that enrich American society. Each wave of immigrant families adds a new chapter to the ongoing immigration story.

However, our current immigration system remains fragmented and problematic. With increasing deportations, stringent border policies, and a complex visa system, many find themselves caught in a web of bureaucracy. This brings us to the pivotal question: how did we arrive at this broken immigration system?

An Overview of Current Issues

Today, debates about immigration often fuel deep divisions within our society. Policies can swing dramatically with changes in administration, leaving many people uncertain about their status and future. This instability affects not only immigrants but also the communities that embrace them. While some may champion strict immigration policies as a means of protecting jobs or national security, others see these measures as inhumane and counterproductive, leading to suffering and family separations.

As we traverse the history of immigration, it becomes clear that to tackle our current challenges, we must learn from the past. Understanding the complexities and contradictions of our immigration journey is essential. How can we create a system that acknowledges our rich history while addressing the needs and concerns of today's society?

Conclusion: A Call to Action

In the chapters that follow, we will dive deeper into the personal narratives of those navigating our broken system. We'll explore their dreams, struggles, and resilience, showcasing the individuals who embody the very essence of the immigrant experience. By bringing these stories to the forefront, we hope to foster compassion and a sense of shared humanity.

Join us as we embark on this exploration together, aiming to better understand our immigration system from multiple perspectives and working toward solutions that honor the legacy of our past while building a more inclusive future.

Chapter 2: The People Behind the Policies: Immigrant Stories

Throughout history, the fabric of American society has been woven by the experiences of countless immigrants. Each individual and family brings a unique story that reflects their hopes, fears, and dreams. These narratives are not just background noise; they are the heartbeats of a system often seen through the detached lens of statistics and political discourse. In this chapter, we will dive into the lives of several immigrants, exploring their journeys and the realities they face within our broken immigration system.

Stories of Hope and Resilience

Maria, a young woman from El Salvador, dreamed of a better life. Like many, she faced violence and poverty in her homeland, leading her to make an agonizing decision. After losing her brother to gang violence, she fled to the U.S. with her young daughter, seeking safety and stability. Maria's journey was fraught with danger, from crossing borders to facing the harsh realities of life as an undocumented immigrant. Despite the constant fear of deportation, Maria found strength in her determination to provide her daughter with a better future. She took on multiple jobs, often working late into the night, all while attending classes to learn English.

Maria's story reflects the resilience that many immigrants possess. Just like her, thousands navigate a complicated maze of legal procedures, uncertain job prospects, and emotional turmoil. Every day, they must balance their aspirations for a brighter future with the daunting challenges of an immigration system that often feels unforgiving.

A Family Torn Apart

James and Sarah, a couple from Nigeria, arrived in the U.S. seeking asylum. They faced persecution in their home country due to their activism for human rights. After a difficult journey, replete with threats to their lives, they managed to reach America, where they thought they would finally find safety. However, their struggles were far from over.

Despite having compelling reasons for their asylum claim, James and Sarah faced a lengthy legal process. They lived in fear, awaiting a decision that kept them in limbo for years. The emotional toll was immense, leading to anxiety and uncertainty about their future. Their children, born in the

U.S., battled with identity issues while trying to comprehend why their parents faced such obstacles.

James and Sarah's story reveals the significant emotional and psychological impact of our immigration system. Families are left feeling isolated and uncertain as they wait for decisions that will determine their fate.

The Young Dreamers

A few hundred miles away in Chicago lives Luis, a young man who arrived in the U.S. as a child. His family came seeking opportunities, and they entered the country without documentation. Growing up in America, Luis faced hurdles due to his status, struggling with the knowledge that he could be deported at any moment.

Luis is just one of many Dreamers—an informal term for undocumented immigrants who arrived in the U.S. as children. They grew up in American culture, often speaking only English and feeling more American than the countries of their birth. The challenge for Luis was not only the fear of deportation but also the complexities of education and employment options.

Despite the challenges, Luis's story highlights hope. He became involved in advocacy, working with organizations to bring attention to the plight of undocumented youth. His passion for social justice has motivated him to fight for change, not just for himself but for others in similar situations.

Bridging the Cultural Divide

Selima, a refugee from Afghanistan, offers another perspective on the immigration experience. When the Taliban regained power, her family was forced to escape. They arrived in the U.S. with little more than the clothes on their backs. Selima faced cultural assimilation challenges, adjusting to a new language and way of life while grappling with the trauma of leaving her homeland.

However, what stands out in Selima's story is her commitment to bridging cultural divides. She enrolled in local community programs to connect with both immigrants and native-born Americans, fostering dialogue and understanding. Through sharing her experiences, she hopes to create empathy and dispel stereotypes surrounding Muslim immigrants.

Common Threads in Immigrant Lives

As we reflect on these stories, certain themes emerge. Many immigrants arrive filled with hope despite the daunting circumstances they face. The enduring desire for safety, opportunity, and a chance to work toward dreams binds these individuals together. Their journeys represent the courage required to navigate an immigration system filled with obstacles.

While the experiences of immigrants vary widely, ranging from those seeking asylum from political violence to others in search of economic opportunities, they share common humanity and resilience. These narratives underscore the importance of examining immigration policies through a compassionate lens, focusing on real people rather than abstract figures.

Conclusion: The Need for Empathy

In uncovering the stories behind the policies, we remember that immigration is ultimately about people—families striving for a better tomorrow, individuals seeking safety, and communities rich with diverse backgrounds. These are the stories that truly matter.

In the following chapters, we will continue to explore these individual experiences while delving deeper into the complexities of the immigration process. By understanding the lives affected by these policies, we can work toward creating a more just and compassionate system that recognizes the invaluable contributions immigrants make to our society.

Chapter 3: Navigating the Maze: Understanding the Immigration Process

Navigating the immigration process in the United States is like putting together a giant puzzle without a clear picture on the box. The rules are complicated, the forms are numerous, and the timeline is often uncertain. In this chapter, we will break down the immigration process, simplifying it into bite-sized pieces and helping to demystify the legal journey that many immigrants must endure.

The Basics of Immigration

At its core, immigration refers to the act of moving to another country to live permanently or temporarily. In the U.S., this can happen through various pathways, each with its own set of rules. Common pathways include family sponsorships, employment-based visas, asylum claims, and refugee status—each resembling a different road on the immigration highway.

<u>Family Sponsorships</u>

Family reunification is a significant priority in the U.S. immigration system. Citizens and lawful permanent residents can sponsor relatives for visas, allowing families to stay together. However, not all family members are eligible. For instance, while spouses and children are often given priority, siblings and adult children face longer wait times and more obstacles.

The process begins with the U.S. citizen or permanent resident filing a petition for their family member. Once approved, the family member must apply for a visa, which includes submitting various documents and undergoing background checks. The wait time can vary drastically, depending on the family relationship and the country of origin. For some families, years can pass before they are reunited.

Employment-Based Visas

Another pathway is through employment-based visas, which allow U.S. businesses to employ foreign workers. There are several categories, ranging from temporary work visas to permanent resident programs like the EB-2 and EB-3 visas. Each category has its eligibility requirements and a maximum number of visas available per year, which creates a competitive and sometimes lengthy process.

The first step for an employment visa typically involves an employer filing a petition with U.S. Citizenship and Immigration Services (USCIS). The process includes labor certification, which requires the employer to demonstrate that there are no qualified U.S. workers available for the position.

The Asylum Process

For individuals fleeing persecution or violence, seeking asylum provides another option. Asylum is a form of protection granted to people in the U.S. who demonstrate a credible fear of returning to their home country due to persecution based on race, religion, nationality, membership in a particular social group, or political opinion.

The asylum process can be lengthy and arduous. After arriving in the U.S., an asylum seeker has one year to file their application. This involves completing extensive paperwork, providing evidence of threats in their home country, and attending interviews. The outcome can result in either a grant of asylum, allowing the individual to stay, or a denial that may lead to deportation.

The Challenges of the Immigration Process

The complexity of the immigration process can lead to significant challenges for many individuals. Language barriers, financial constraints, and a lack of understanding of the legal system often make the journey overwhelming. For example, navigating the long list of forms and documents required can be exhausting and confusing.

Moreover, many immigrants don't have access to legal assistance, which can further complicate their cases. Legal help can be costly, and finding reputable immigration lawyers can feel like searching for a needle in a haystack. Unfortunately, without proper guidance, many individuals make errors that can result in delays, denials, or even deportation.

Real-Life Examples

Let's take a closer look at two contrasting stories that exemplify the challenges individuals face.

Alejandro's Path

Alejandro fled violence in Honduras and arrived in the U.S. seeking asylum. He spent years in his home country living in fear for his life, eventually deciding to leave. After a harrowing journey through Mexico, he arrived at the U.S. border, where he believed he would find safety.

Upon filing for asylum, Alejandro was overwhelmed by the intricate process. He struggled with language barriers and often felt intimidated by the system. Despite these challenges, he persisted, drawing strength from the support of local advocacy groups. With their help, he eventually submitted a strong application, detailing his history and fears. His persistence paid off when he was granted asylum, allowing him to start anew and pursue his education.

Rachel's Story

In contrast, Rachel, a young woman from the Philippines, faced a different set of challenges. Her parents had sponsored her to come to the U.S. as a student, but she became immediately confused by the bureaucracy. She encountered difficulties securing the necessary documents and faced expensive tuition rates at her college.

Despite her parents' support, Rachel struggled to find information about her visa status and the path to permanent residency. Frustrated and anxious, she fell into a common trap where misinformation about her options led to missed deadlines and, ultimately, a denial of her application to stay in the U.S.

Rachel's story illustrates a tragic outcome that can occur due to the opaque nature of the immigration process. With the right information and guidance, her situation could have unfolded more positively.

The Role of Advocacy Groups

As both Alejandro's and Rachel's stories suggest, advocacy groups play a crucial role in helping immigrants navigate the complex landscape of U.S. immigration.

Organizations like the Immigrant Legal Resource Center and the American Immigration Council work tirelessly to provide legal assistance, education, and resources to those seeking help.

These groups often hold workshops, offer free legal consultations, and help individuals fill out forms. They also advocate for policy changes, striving to create a more humane and accessible immigration system. Even modest support from these organizations can lead to significant positive outcomes, moving immigrants closer to their dreams.

Conclusion: A Call for Change

Understanding the immigration process is essential, not just for immigrants but for the communities that host them. By demystifying the complexities, we can foster empathy and advocate for reforms that simplify the pathway to citizenship and residency.

The immigration process is not just a bureaucratic maze; it represents the hopes and dreams of countless individuals and families striving for a better future.

In the next chapter, we will delve into the human cost of our immigration policies, focusing on families torn apart by bureaucracy and misunderstandings. These stories reveal the emotional toll of a system that, while intended to protect and regulate, can often lead to devastating consequences.

Chapter 4: The Human Cost: Families Torn Apart

At the heart of the immigration debate lie the real stories of families. Each statistic represents not just numbers but lives intertwined by love, dreams, and hope. Yet, the harsh reality is that many families are torn apart by the very system designed to unite them. In this chapter, we will explore the emotional, psychological, and financial toll of immigration policies that separate families and the impact it has on individuals, parents, and children alike.

A Fractured Family

Consider the story of Daniela, a mother from Guatemala. She fled her country with her young son, Javier, after her husband was murdered by gang members. Seeking safety and a chance at a better life, Daniela and Javier made the treacherous journey to the United States. Their dream was simple: to find safety and build a new life together. However, upon arriving, their hope quickly turned into chaos.

Even after enduring the perilous journey, Daniela found herself facing a heart-wrenching decision. While her initial intent was to seek asylum, she was soon swept into the complexities of the immigration system. After an arduous process, she fell victim to a detention center due to a paperwork error. Tragically, mother and son were separated, plunging them into a nightmare of uncertainty and fear.

The Psychological Impact of Separation

The emotional and psychological impacts of separation are profound. For Javier, being separated from his mother meant enduring loneliness, confusion, and deep emotional scars. Young children like him often struggle to understand why their parents are not around and live under the constant shadow of uncertainty.

Research has shown that children who experience such separations often face long-term developmental challenges. Javier found it hard to focus in school and struggled to make friends. The trauma of his separation was compounded by worries about his mother's safety and future.

And for Daniela, the experience of separation led to depression and anxiety. Every day spent apart from her son felt like a lifetime. She was left to navigate the cold, bureaucratic maze of immigration hearings without the one person she was fighting for. The price paid for pursuing safety was an unbearable fracture in their relationship.

The Ripple Effects on Families

Daniela and Javier's story illustrates a broader issue experienced by countless families. Many immigrants are caught in a system where family reunification is nearly impossible, creating rifts that can last years or even a lifetime. Other families, like that of immigration activist Angela, also found themselves navigating heartbreaking challenges.

Angela, a U.S. citizen, worked tirelessly to help her undocumented migrant husband, Jose, after he was detained during a routine traffic stop. He was a devoted father to their two young children. The family was torn apart during a crucial time in their lives. Angela felt the weight of raising their children alone while also fighting a legal battle for her husband's release. The kids missed their father deeply, and this emotional gap created tension and anxiety at home. Angela had to balance holding together her family while working multiple jobs to make ends meet.

The emotional toll on Angela's entire family was enormous. Their home transformed from one filled with laughter and unity to one laden with worry and sorrow. The children didn't understand why their father was gone, often blaming themselves or feeling ashamed of his absence.

The Complexity of Family Reunification

Family reunification in the U.S. immigration system is often hindered by policy. Visa backlogs, complex legal requirements, and strict eligibility criteria create an environment where families are often waiting for years to be together again.

For families like Daniela and Angela's, the stakes couldn't be higher. The emotional struggles many endure while separated can lead to irreparable damage to family bonds. Children who are separated from their parents may struggle with relationships later in life, creating generational cycles of trauma.

Additionally, when families do manage to reunite after long separations, they often find themselves having to rebuild their relationships from scratch. The dynamics have changed; children grow and mature, and parents may not always return to the same roles they once played. These adjustments can lead to frustration, misunderstandings, and resentment, complicating already fragile bonds.

The Role of Organizations and Support Systems

To combat the effects of family separation, several organizations tirelessly advocate for families caught in the immigration system. These groups, such as the Families Belong Together coalition, work to raise awareness and bring attention to the emotional impact of these policies.

They provide resources, emotional support, and legal assistance to families navigating the immigration maze. Groups working to reunite families can offer counseling, legal representation, and other support services that help families transition through these challenges.

While systemic change is crucial, these organizations play an essential role in aiding families during their most vulnerable moments. They amplify Voices unheard and provide vital resources to those who may otherwise feel powerless.

A Call for Awareness and Change

As we reflect on the stories of families like Daniela and Angela's, it becomes critical to advocate for changes in the immigration system that prioritize family unity. Policies need to evolve to address the emotional and psychological impacts of separation and to ensure that families can stay together as they pursue safety and new beginnings.

The current immigration climate can dehumanize individuals, reducing them to mere statistics in a political debate.

However, by sharing these human stories, we remind ourselves that behind policies are families who deserve compassion, empathy, and understanding.

Our immigration system should prioritize keeping families intact, recognizing the importance of stability and security in the lives of individuals and their loved ones.

In the next chapter, we will explore the experiences of refugees and asylum seekers, diving into their stories of courage and resilience as they flee from danger in search of safety in the U.S. Their journeys highlight the pressing need for humane policies that prioritize the well-being of those seeking refuge from persecution and violence.

Chapter 5: Refugees and Asylum Seekers: Seeking Safety

When we think of refugees and asylum seekers, we often imagine distant lands filled with turmoil and strife. What we sometimes forget is that these individuals are real people with hopes, dreams, and family members left behind in the pursuit of safety. In this chapter, we will delve into the journeys of refugees and asylum seekers, exploring the unique challenges they face in navigating the U.S. immigration system and the emotional toll that comes with seeking safety.

Defining Refugees and Asylum Seekers

To understand the experiences of refugees and asylum seekers, we must first clarify the difference between the two. Refugees are individuals forced to flee their country due to a well-founded fear of persecution based on race, religion, nationality, political opinion, or membership in a particular social group. They apply for refugee status while still in their home country or through temporary camps.

Asylum seekers, on the other hand, are individuals who have already entered the U.S. and are seeking protection after arriving. Their claims are made based on similar circumstances of persecution. While both refugees and asylum seekers share the common goal of finding safety, the paths they take to achieve that goal can vary dramatically.

The Journey of Refugees

Many refugees come from war-torn regions where their lives and the lives of their loved ones are in constant danger. Take the story of Fatima, a young woman from Syria. As the conflict escalated, she found herself in a situation where her family was targeted due to their moderate political beliefs. After losing her brother to violence, Fatima made the difficult decision to flee, hoping to find safety for herself and her remaining family members.

fatima's journey to the U.S. was long and perilous, with treacherous border crossings, threats from human traffickers, and an overwhelming fear of being caught. She traveled through several countries before finally arriving in the U.S., where she would begin the arduous process of seeking asylum.

The Asylum Process

Upon arriving in the U.S., Fatima faced a maze of paperwork and requirements just to start her asylum claim. She was given a limited time frame within which to file her application, and the pressure weighed heavily on her. The process included filling out complex forms and gathering evidence to prove her claims of persecution.

Fatima's experience reflects a broader trend among asylum seekers who encounter a system marred by complications. Many struggle to navigate the legal jargon and requirements without assistance, risking denials that can lead to deportation.

Moreover, language barriers often hinder effective communication with legal representatives. Fatima struggled to articulate her traumatic experiences in English during interviews, leading to anxiety and frustration. Stories like hers highlight the importance of providing language access and legal support to those in need.

Facing Uncertainty

Unlike refugees, asylum seekers often find themselves living in uncertainty for extended periods while their cases are being reviewed. U.S. immigration courts can be overwhelmed, leading to long backlogs and waiting times that can stretch years. During this time, individuals must navigate the difficulties of life in a new country while carrying the weight of their traumatic pasts.

Many asylum seekers are left in limbo, forced to rely on temporary work permits that allow them to work and support themselves. However, this can be a constant source of anxiety. For example, Fatima struggled with finding stable employment due to her transitional status, all while worrying about her family still in Syria. The isolation and uncertainty can become overwhelming, leading to depression and anxiety—common issues among refugees and asylum seekers.

The Role of Community and Support Networks

Community organizations play a vital role in supporting refugees and asylum seekers throughout this challenging process. Groups like the International Rescue Committee and local refugee resettlement organizations help newcomers integrate into their communities. They offer resources, job training, language classes, and emotional support, making a crucial difference in their lives.

Fatima found solace in a local refugee support group where she connected with others who had faced similar challenges. The support group became a safe space for her to share her experiences and fears. With the group's help, she was able to access legal resources and find a job within her community.

These organizations are essential in creating a safety net for those navigating the complex immigration process. They help foster a sense of belonging and provide practical support as refugees adapt to their new lives.

The Need for Policy Reform

As we examine the experiences of refugees and asylum seekers, we realize the urgent need for reforming the immigration system to ensure these individuals receive fair and humane treatment. Current policies often prioritize speed and efficiency over humanity, leaving vulnerable individuals to navigate an intricate and unfriendly labyrinth of bureaucracy.

Streamlined processes, better legal representation, and access to mental health resources are necessary changes to facilitate the integration of refugees and asylum seekers. Addressing the complexities and nuances of their journeys is vital in creating a system that genuinely protects those seeking safety in the U.S.

Conclusion: A Humanitarian Perspective

The stories of refugees and asylum seekers remind us of the importance of compassion and understanding in addressing these issues. Behind every statistic lies a person; behind every policy is a story. As we continue this exploration of our broken immigration system, we can advocate for inclusive policies that recognize the dignity and humanity of all seeking refuge.

In the next chapter, we will explore the economic impact of immigration, particularly the vital role immigrants play in the U.S. workforce. By examining their contributions, we will further emphasize the importance of inclusive immigration policies that benefit both individuals and society as a whole.

Chapter 6: The Economic Impact: Immigrants in the Workforce

When discussing immigration, one of the most commonly debated topics is the economic impact immigrants have on the U.S. workforce. Myths and misconceptions abound, often portraying immigrants as job stealers or burdens on the economy. However, the reality tells a different story. In this chapter, we will explore the crucial role immigrants play in enhancing the workforce, contributing to the economy, and driving innovation.

The Diverse Contributions of Immigrants

Immigrants come from various backgrounds and possess a wide range of skills. They fill key jobs across different sectors, from agriculture to technology. According to the American Immigration Council, immigrants make up about 18% of the U.S. workforce, significantly contributing to key industries, including healthcare, construction, and hospitality.

Take the story of Ravi, a software engineer from India. After earning his degree, he moved to the U.S. on a work visa, drawn by the vibrant tech industry and opportunities for growth. Ravi quickly landed a job at a leading tech company, where he began making substantial contributions to projects that enhanced productivity and innovation.

Ravi's journey is not unique. Many immigrants bring advanced degrees, specialized skills, and a wealth of experience, filling critical gaps in the labor market. Particularly in fields like healthcare, immigrants make up a significant proportion of doctors, nurses, and caregivers, providing essential services to the community.

The Agricultural Sector

In the agricultural industry, immigrants play an even more vital role. Many farms rely on seasonal immigrant labor to plant, harvest, and pack crops. Without this workforce, our food supply would struggle to meet the demand. For instance, studies have shown that more than 70% of farm workers in the U.S. are immigrants, often working long hours in challenging conditions to keep the agricultural sector afloat.

The story of Maria, a migrant farmworker from Mexico, exemplifies this reality. Each season, she travels to different states in search of work, picking fruits and vegetables to support her family. Her hard work ensures that fresh produce makes it to grocery stores across America. Without the contributions of farmworkers like Maria, prices for fresh produce would soar, and many crops would go unharvested.

Economic Contributions Beyond Jobs

The impact of immigrants on the U.S. economy extends beyond filling jobs; they also contribute significantly through taxes and consumer spending. According to the Institute on Taxation and Economic Policy, undocumented immigrants alone pay an estimated $11.74 billion in state and local taxes each year.

These contributions are vital for funding public services like education and healthcare, helping to sustain communities —in fact, immigrants are already paying into systems that often deny them benefits. A many-fold multiplier effect comes into play as workers spend their wages on goods and services, stimulating local economies and creating jobs for everyone.

Innovation and Entrepreneurship

In addition to contributing to the labor market, immigrants play a critical role in driving innovation and entrepreneurship in the U.S. About one-quarter of new businesses are founded by immigrants, including household names like Google, Tesla, and Intel.

Entrepreneurs like Sarah, a refugee from Syria, embody this spirit of innovation. Upon resettling in the U.S., she harnessed her passion for cooking and launched a successful catering business that celebrates her culture. Not only has she provided for her family, but she has also created jobs for others, enhancing the local economy and fostering cultural exchange.

Studies have shown that immigrant entrepreneurs contribute significantly to job creation. By starting new businesses, they not only feed their dreams but also invigorate local economies, creating jobs for both immigrants and native-born citizens.

Dispelling Myths about Immigration

Despite the clear contributions of immigrants to the U.S. economy, myths and misinformation persist. Many people believe immigrants take away jobs from native-born workers or negatively impact wages. However, research consistently shows that immigration tends to complement rather than compete with the native workforce.

A study from the National Academies of Sciences, Engineering, and Medicine found that immigration has a net positive effect on the economy, contributing to overall economic growth while having minimal effects on wages for native workers. Immigrants often fill labor shortages in lower-skilled jobs that many native workers are unwilling to accept, allowing businesses to thrive while creating additional jobs.

The Importance of Inclusive Immigration Policies

Recognizing the economic contributions of immigrants emphasizes the importance of creating inclusive immigration policies that allow for greater workforce participation. Policies that encourage skilled labor, support family reunification, and streamline the immigration process can enhance economic growth and ensure the continual contributions of immigrants to society.

Advocating for pathways to legal status for undocumented immigrants can also lead to significant economic benefits. By granting them legal status, they would gain the opportunity to work more freely, contribute fully to the economy, and potentially start their businesses, all resulting in a more dynamic workforce.

Conclusion: Immigrants as Economic Contributors

The stories of immigrants in the workforce reveal a rich tapestry of contributions that strengthen and drive the U.S. economy. While misconceptions often cast a shadow over the realities of immigration, it's essential to amplify these voices and highlight their positive impact on society.

As we continue our exploration of the broken immigration system, we will focus on the ongoing advocacy for reform in Chapter 7. By examining various organizations and initiatives working toward change, we can better understand how individuals can mobilize and create a more equitable system for all.

Chapter 7: Paths to Change: Advocacy and Reform

As we have learned throughout this book, the U.S. immigration system is riddled with complexities, misunderstandings, and often, heartbreak. Thankfully, many individuals and organizations are tirelessly working to advocate for meaningful reforms that aim to transform this broken system into one that is just, equitable, and compassionate. In this chapter, we will explore the various paths to change, highlighting advocacy efforts, community initiatives, and the roles individuals can play in shaping immigration policies.

Advocacy Groups Leading the Charge

Across the country, numerous advocacy organizations are committed to addressing the challenges faced by immigrants. These organizations focus on everything from legal representation to policy reform, helping to amplify the voices of those often overlooked in the immigration debate.

One pioneering organization, the American Civil Liberties Union (ACLU), works to defend the rights of immigrants, advocating for fair treatment in the legal system and pushing back against discriminatory policies. They have successfully challenged harmful laws and practices in court, highlighting the need for a more humane approach to immigration.

Another key player in immigration advocacy is the National Immigration Law Center (NILC), which seeks to defend and advance the rights of low-income immigrants. NILC provides legal resources, research, and policy analysis, ensuring that vulnerable populations have access to the support they need. Their work is critical in shaping laws that promote fairness and equality.

Organizations like United We Dream focus on empowering young undocumented immigrants, known as Dreamers. They advocate for policies such as the Deferred Action for Childhood Arrivals (DACA) program, which allows some undocumented individuals brought to the U.S. as children to live and work lawfully. Through grassroots organizing and community engagement, they mobilize young voices to advocate for comprehensive immigration reform.

The Legislative Path to Reform

While grassroots advocacy is essential, the legislative process is a critical component of enacting meaningful change. Recent years have seen calls for comprehensive immigration reform, with many advocating for policies that prioritize family reunification, pathways to citizenship for undocumented immigrants, and protections for asylum seekers.

However, navigating the political landscape can be challenging. Immigration reform is often a contentious issue, leading to partisan disagreements that stall progress.

As a result, advocates emphasize the need for public support and engagement, urging individuals to contact their representatives and advocate for policies that reflect their values.

The Power of Community Initiatives

In addition to advocacy at the national level, local communities are taking action to create change. Across the U.S., community organizations are stepping up to provide support and resources for immigrants, building resilience within vulnerable populations.

For instance, many cities offer sanctuary policies aimed at providing safe spaces for immigrant communities. These policies seek to protect undocumented individuals from ICE raids and deportations, allowing them to live without constant fear. Local organizations facilitate resources, access to legal support, and community networks that help immigrants thrive.

Cultural and educational initiatives also play a vital role. Programs that celebrate the contributions of immigrant communities, such as cultural festivals and language classes, foster solidarity and understanding among residents. As community members come together, they create a stronger network of support paving the way for positive change.

The Importance of Grassroots Movements

In recent years, grassroots movements have gained momentum, mobilizing large segments of the population to advocate for immigration reform. The rise of social media has amplified these efforts, enabling advocates to share their stories, mobilize supporters, and raise awareness about the challenges immigrants face.

Movements like Families Belong Together, which gained significant traction during the controversial family separation policy, have united millions around the cause of immigrant justice. By bringing immigrants' stories to the forefront, these movements build solidarity and push back against harmful policies.

Empowering Individuals to Make a Difference

Advocacy isn't limited to organizations and large movements; individuals can also play a crucial role in driving change. Here are some ways people can contribute:

1. **Educate Yourself**: Understanding the complexities of the immigration system helps demystify the issues. By learning the facts, individuals can better advocate for reforms.

2. **Raise Awareness**: Sharing stories on social media, writing blog posts, or speaking at local meetings can raise awareness about the immigration crisis.

3. **Attend Community Meetings**: Engaging with local organizations allows individuals to contribute their voice and share their experiences.

4. **Support Immigrant-Friendly Policies**: Contacting local elected officials and advocating for policies that support immigrant communities can help drive change at the legislative level.

5. **Volunteer**: Many organizations need volunteers to assist with legal support, community outreach, or fundraising. These contributions can make a meaningful difference.

The Future of Immigration Advocacy

As we look to the future, various paths for reform remain. With shifting political climates and changing public attitudes, there is potential for progress. Continued advocacy ensures that the voices of immigrants will be amplified, and their stories will be central to discussions about our broken immigration system.

Together, we can cultivate a more just and equitable system that recognizes the inherent humanity of all individuals, regardless of their immigration status.

In our final chapter, we will discuss what an inclusive future might look like—how we can envision a world where immigration processes are fair, humane, and supportive of families seeking opportunities and safety.

Chapter 8: A Brighter Future: Building an Inclusive System

As we reach the conclusion of our exploration into the broken immigration system, we must take a moment to envision what a brighter future could look like for immigrants and communities across the United States. This future is not just a dream; it is a goal that we can work toward collectively. In this chapter, we will discuss the essential components of an inclusive immigration system, highlighting reforms that prioritize humanity, dignity, and the values that define us as a nation.

A Blueprint for Reform

To create a more just immigration system, we must focus on several key areas of reform:

1. **Streamlined Pathways to Citizenship**: A more accessible path to

citizenship for undocumented immigrants is crucial. Comprehensive legislation should provide clear and fair pathways for individuals who have contributed to society and have roots in their communities. By allowing individuals to apply for legal status, we can foster a sense of belonging and stability within immigrant communities.

2. **Protecting Family Unity**: Immigration policies should prioritize keeping families together. Current regulations often create unnecessary barriers to family reunification. By simplifying the application processes and ensuring timely processing, we can help families avoid long separations, ensuring that loved ones can support one another.

3. **Humane Treatment of Asylum Seekers and Refugees**: The U.S. must commit to humane treatment of refugees and asylum seekers. This includes providing adequate resources for legal support, ensuring fair and timely adjudication of claims, and fostering an environment that welcomes those fleeing violence and persecution. We can create safer pathways for individuals seeking refuge, emphasizing our commitment to human rights.

4. **Combating Discrimination**: Policies must actively combat discrimination and prejudice against immigrants. Education and community outreach programs can help dispel myths and foster a more inclusive attitude toward immigrants in society. Promoting cultural exchange and understanding

can bridge gaps and build solidarity among residents.

5. **Acknowledging Economic Contributions**: Recognizing the economic contributions of immigrants is vital in shaping public opinion and policy. By highlighting the success stories of immigrant entrepreneurs and workers, we can shift the narrative around immigration, emphasizing the benefits they bring to our economy and culture.

The Role of Community Engagement

In building an inclusive system, individual and community engagement is essential. As we have seen through various advocacy initiatives, grassroots movements can lead to substantive change. This requires ongoing support from individuals, not just organizations.

By actively participating in local advocacy efforts, attending town hall meetings, and connecting with immigrant communities, individuals can help shape a positive narrative around immigration. Engaging in honest conversations, sharing personal stories, and building relationships can create empathy and understanding among diverse groups.

Areas of Hope and Opportunity

Despite the challenges facing our immigration system, there are areas of hope and opportunity that can lead us toward a more positive future. Amidst renewed discussions about immigration reform, public awareness and activism are growing. The increasing visibility of immigrant voices, paired with the stories of hardship and resilience, is paving the way for meaningful change.

Emerging leaders from immigrant communities are stepping forward to advocate for not only themselves but also for their neighbors. Empowerment initiatives encourage young individuals, including Dreamers, to take action and become the voices of their communities. The power of storytelling continues to resonate, creating connections and driving the narrative toward compassion and humanity.

Moving Forward Together

To achieve a brighter future in immigration policy, we must work together. Engaging with our neighbors, participating in community initiatives, and advocating for change at the local and national levels create the momentum needed to drive reform. Everyone has a role to play, whether through volunteering, being informed, or speaking out against injustice.

Together, we can cultivate a society where individuals can pursue their dreams—unburdened by fear or hostility. By promoting the values of dignity, respect, and inclusion, we can begin to heal the fractures in our immigration system.

Conclusion: A Vision for Tomorrow

In envisioning a brighter future, we reinforce the notion that immigration is not just a political issue; it's a deeply personal one rooted in love, aspirations, and the pursuit of a better life. By advocating for systemic change and supporting immigrants in their journeys, we honor their resilience and validate their struggles.

While the path may not always be clear, the collective efforts of individuals, organizations, and communities hold the potential for transformative change. Together, we can craft an immigration system that reflects the fundamental values of justice, compassion, and humanity—one that opens the door to opportunity for all individuals seeking a place to call home.

As we conclude this journey through our broken immigration system, let's carry forward the stories we've uncovered and commit to working towards a more inclusive and equitable future, where every individual has the chance to thrive and belong.